Day Trading Strategies

Learn All Fundamentals To Trade With Success. Day Trading Psychology And Risk Management Techniques To Make Profit For A Live

MATTHEW R. HILL AND HENRY KRATTER

Table of Contents

Introduction

A swing trader doesn't need to sit at his computer watching the stock markets all day long, although you certainly can if that's an option for you and you like doing it. Swing traders can also start small and grow their business over time.

While substantial profits are attainable, it's not a get-rich-quick scheme and although it can be done on a part-time basis, we want you to start thinking of swing trading as a business from this point forward. The goal is to earn profits, and you can use those profits as ordinary income if you like or reinvest them to build your retirement account or some combination of the two. That is entirely up to you. But keep in mind one thing: very few people are going to make a millions in their first year and slide into retirement.

With these good intentions in mind, we will give you, through the course of this book, profound advice on trading strategies, capital preservation, risk management, and position sizing. But it isn't all doom and gloom because we will also show you how to identify emerging high-performing stocks and when and where to enter and exit a trade so that you optimize your profits. We will also show you how to lock-in your profits while you continue to ride the wave to even greater profits.

Swing Trading is by no means easy, but if you follow the advice in this book you will firmly have put the odds on your side, you will be confident in trading with the correct strategy in the market as well as in balancing your risk and reward dilemma - and you can't really ask for more than that.

Swing trading can be a great way to earn a big profit in a short amount of time to the stock market. Start learning more about swing trading with this guidebook that's designed to provide you with concise information.

Chapter 1: Day Trading Cryptocurrency

What is a cryptocurrency?

A cryptocurrency is a kind of digital asset. It is held electronically (online) and has no physical existence. It primarily functions as a substitute for money. It is secured using the technology known as **cryptography**. Cryptography refers to the practice of securing information by converting it into codes. It was extensively used during the Second World War. At that time, it was important for the military to ensure that their communication with one another was secured and protected against the enemy. This only goes to show how much you can trust and depend on this technology.

To date, there are more than 1,000 cryptocurrencies being traded in the market. Still, only a few of them can attract the interest of the people and can gain significant value. Among all the cryptocurrencies being traded, the number one and most successful cryptocurrency is Bitcoin. As of January 11, 2018, the price of 1 bitcoin is around $14,520 USD.

Cryptocurrencies are not considered as fiat money. What is **fiat money**? Fiat money refers to the official currency of a state. A good example of fiat money is the US dollar. Since these aren't considered as such, these are also not considered as legal tender. Legal tender refers to that which a debtor can compel his/her creditor to accept payment. Of course, the exception here is if payment in cryptocurrency is also stipulated in the contract. It is noteworthy that even though cryptocurrencies aren't considered as fiat money and legal tender, there are still many individuals and merchants around the world who accept cryptocurrencies as a medium of payments, such as Overdrive, Microsoft, Steam, Virgin Galactic, Peach Airlines, and Tesla, among many others.

Cryptocurrency users also enjoy anonymity. In a cryptocurrency transaction, only the cryptocurrency wallet address and the amount involved are usually revealed. Other information as to the name, address, and other personal details of the parties involved remain confidential.

The Most Common Types of Cryptocurrencies

Unlike what many beginners think, there are more cryptocurrencies than just Bitcoin. And in future, more will come up.

However, you are right if you only know of Bitcoin because it's way ahead of the pack. It is most popular; it started this wonderful technological revolution. So, Bitcoin it is!

You see, a name for the other cryptocurrencies has been coined and they are collectively referred to as altcoins or alternative coins.

Without any centralized authority over the Bitcoin, need we say that it has practically set the trends for most other cryptocurrencies in the market? The other coins come in such a way as if they are the enhanced versions of Bitcoin, but the truth is that if Bitcoin were not here, they too would not be here.

Although, currently there are more than 1000 cryptocurrencies, in the future, this number can go up. But Bitcoin will remain way ahead of the pack, being the most preferred coin in the world as it's backed by perfect technology.

So, with so many cryptocurrencies in the market, well, what others are worth your attention? Well, take your pick from the few presented below:

Ethereum

In your search for information online, you will find Ethereum mentioned in many circles. This is another type of digital money technology, decentralized and made to run without any form of interference, control or fraud.

However, the most interesting part of it is the Ether – a cryptographic token that is used by developers to codify, secure and run applications (other than money) on the Ethereum platform.

It is the second after Bitcoin in terms of value and distribution and over time, Ethereum has today become the technology of choice for many people as it can be used to encrypt anything, codify, trade and do much more in a very decentralized manner.

Only a few years in the market since it was released in 2015, Ethereum is worth looking into if you would like to diversify your cryptocurrency portfolio.

Litecoin

Called LTC, Litecoin has been a good number of years in the market and is today regarded as second only to Bitcoin.

It's perfect for you if you would like to diversify your coin portfolio.

It's built on the same concept as Bitcoin, that is, decentralized, peer-to-peer computer networking, storage and backup and most importantly, it uses a technology called Scrypt for security. This technology can be decoded by consumer grade CPUs thus making it possible for everyone to invest in Litecoin.

There are caps designed to keep Litecoin safe from inflation. For example, it is said that the value of Litecoin in the market cannot exceed $84 million. This is designed to keep it scarce, attractive and valuable for a good number of years.

Who uses Litecoin? Like Bitcoin, the list of international merchants who accept Litecoin continues to grow. Apart from that, developers and software vendors have no qualms at all about being paid with LTC.

BitcoinCash

While this is not exactly Bitcoin despite the relationship in names, it is a nice investment that is coming up very fast. It is largely used by the Bitcoin enthusiasts, but it isn't expected to rise too high.

Dogecoin

Would you believe this coin was created just for fun and then when it was released, it was found it had some staying power? It is not supposed to do as well as Bitcoin, but it is in many features identical to Litecoin.

If you are a true Cryptocurrency enthusiast, maybe you can add several Dogecoin coins into your portfolio.

Namecoin

This is regarded as same as Bitcoin because initially, it was designed to be an upgrade of Bitcoin but later on, it was deemed much better to release it as a standalone coin fearing that it could cause problems if released as an upgrade.

While it is a direct spinoff of Bitcoin, it's still very low in value, only worth about

DarkCoin

A creation of Evan Duffield, this is one of the easiest coins to mine. Although it's not in the same league as Bitcoin, it's still up there in terms of competence and value as Ethereum and Litecoin. Because it requires less mining power, that makes it accessible to a good number of people.

Ripple

Although it is one of the cheapest cryptocurrencies in the market, Ripple has been integrated by some banks thanks to its design and purpose. It was created in 2012 as a remittance network, currency exchange and for gross settlement. With that kind of progress and purpose in the market, this coin will stick around even though it's one of the cheapest in the market today.

Monero

This is perhaps one of the most secure and untraceable cryptocurrencies in the market today. It is so secure and anonymous such that it has been referred to as an anonymous

13

currency. If you would like to make some payments and remain totally unseen on the web, this is the currency for you.

SexCoin

What a name for cryptocurrency and yes, you guessed right, this coin was created to help you stay anonymous if you're a consumer of adult content on the web. Thus, instead of using your credit card or bank wire for paying for such services, you can use the totally private SexCoin.

Blockchain technology

The blockchain technology, or simply **blockchain**, is the backbone technology of bitcoin and other cryptocurrencies. It is defined as a decentralized and public distributed ledger that has a high security. It functions as a repository of cryptocurrency transactions and records. It is public in the sense that all the records on the blockchain are viewable and verifiable by everyone on the network. This gives it a sense of complete transparency. It's also decentralized because there is no central organization or government that has control over it. This ensures fairness and that it's free from any and all forms of undue influence and manipulation. The blockchain technology is composed of records known as **blocks**. Every new block is connected to the block that comes before it using a hash pointer. Hence, all the blocks are interconnected with one another. No block can be altered without affecting all the other blocks on the chain. Also, every update on the blockchain such as when a new block is added will also reflect on all the ledgers as shown to all the users. This is the concept of the distributed ledger. The blockchain technology also has a high security. For an attack against the blockchain to be successful, it has to possess at least 51% of the total hash rate of the entire blockchain. Since the blockchain is spread over a vast network of computers, it's virtually impossible for a hacker to meet the 51% requirement. This makes blockchain virtually invulnerable to attacks. Hence, it is trusted by countless of people worldwide.

The blockchain technology can still be considered a new technology. There is still so much that can be expected from it in the future. It's also noteworthy that this technology is making a name for itself aside from being closely associated with bitcoin and other cryptocurrencies. It has been found that this technology can be used for purposes other than recording cryptocurrency transactions and beyond the use of financial sectors. Indeed, this technology is something that you should keep an eye on. In fact, even those who aren't in favor of the use of cryptocurrencies find value in blockchain technology.

Supply and Demand

When it comes to deciding on a cryptocurrency to invest in, it is important to remember that the price isn't controlled in any traditional way except by supply and demand. As such, some experts believe that they more fully express the true intent of the market more clearly than fiat currencies. The one area where they see far more external influence than their compatriots, however, is when it comes to manipulation by speculative investors.

As such, this leads to a pricing bubble that all cryptocurrencies are influenced by to some degree as their prices rises above what the market alone would dictate. This problem is magnified even more in smaller cryptocurrencies as there could only be a few thousand people holding units of it at a given time which means that even a moderate change by one individual could cause ripples across the limited market.

The basic aspects of cryptocurrency trading occur in much the same way as any other type of trading with buyers looking to buy low and sellers looking to sell high. The average smaller cryptocurrency can experience as much as 15 percent movement in its price per day which means the potential for profit, or loss, is significant if the proper caution isn't applied. In fact, because the market as a whole is so speculator-focused it is practically impossible to find a cryptocurrency list on a major exchange that isn't experiencing some extent of pricing bubble.

This is not to say that pricing bubbles are completely without merit, as long as you can get in before things get too out of hand. When buying into any cryptocurrency, this means you're going to need to do some research and determine where the price would likely be at if the market weren't being influenced by speculation. As long as you don't simply follow the crowd in an effort to jump on the next big thing, there is no reason you can't get in early on a cheap cryptocurrency and ride its wave of speculation, making a significant profit in the process.

How Do I Invest in Cryptocurrency?

Before any such question is answered, a more fundamental one might be, "Should I invest in Cryptocurrency?"

Cryptocurrency is the flavor of the month now. The value of Bitcoins has been rising for most of a year. In May 2017, Bitcoin reached $2,000 per coin and rose above $2,500 before declining to $2,400 a coin recently.

If those numbers don't impress you, then consider this: an investment in Bitcoin in 2010 of $100 worth, when each coin was valued at less than a cent would be worth more than $70 million now!

Even if you had purchased some bitcoin in 2016, you would be very pleased. Bitcoin rose approximately 180% during that year. This compares very favorably with the stock market, whose returns ranged between 7.9% and 15%, according to reports.

Other cryptocurrencies beside bitcoin have also done well. As an example, Ethereum, which was launched during 2015, made spectacular gains including one gain of 35% in a 24-hour period. Another Cryptocurrency Litecoin is comparable Bitcoin but is much easier to obtain, easier to use, and regarded as having less value. This year it has gone up 700%!

Does this mean you should purchase Cryptocurrency as soon as possible? Some think so with some proponents expecting its value to keep rising. Some see a Bitcoin reaching a value of $100,000 within ten years. Although digital currencies may appear strange now, it's timely to remember that when Microsoft, Apple and other technology company brands began advancing in the 1980s, some believed there was no use for a personal computer. History has shown that these people were utterly wrong and people who were visionary enough to invest in Microsoft or Apple then are sitting pretty now.

Still, caution and care should be exercised. If the price of an asset is going up, it does not mean its worth is truly increasing. Good examples are found throughout history with a particularly infamous one being U.S. real estate in the late 2000s. Often the things that are driving prices up are lies and exaggeration and if something goes up it generally comes down.

If you wish to purchase and trade Cryptocurrency, then you should first use the exchanges. These sites allow the acquisition and sale of Cryptocurrency with the use of fiat money. Before using an exchange, you need to check how reliable it is and its quality. There are various ways of doing this which include liquidity, fees, limits for purchase and withdrawal, the volume of trades, spread, security, comprehensibility (user-friendliness) and fees.

Why Invest in Cryptocurrency?

People make cryptocurrency investments for various reasons. However, there are three important reasons why you should invest in cryptocurrency. First, investing in cryptocurrency is a way of hedging your assets against the impending fall of the dollar imperium. Cryptocurrency is a wave that is silently revolutionizing money. By investing, you are essentially betting on the success of this revolution. Second, you should only invest if you support the vision behind cryptocurrency – that of universal currency that is free from control by governments. Finally, you should invest in cryptocurrencies only if you understand the technology behind them.

Unfortunately, some people are investing in cryptocurrency because of the fear of missing out (FOMO), in the hopes of making a quick buck. They don't even understand the technology. This is a very bad investment strategy.

17

You should also note that cryptocurrencies aren't like any ordinary investment. They are more volatile than any other investment class. They are unregulated assets. They are also a very high-risk investment. There is always the risk that you lose your key, an exchange or your wallet gets hacked, or they might even get outlawed altogether.

Building Your Portfolio – Which Cryptocurrencies Should You Buy?

For most people, the only cryptocurrency they have thought of investing in is Bitcoin. This is because up until recently, Bitcoin has been the only dominant cryptocurrency. The other altcoins have only been penny stocks with little chance of profitability. Though, things have now changed. While Bitcoin remains dominant, its share in the cryptocurrency market has dropped to around 40%, down from 90%. This is mostly as a result of the growth of Ethereum as well as the scalability problems facing Bitcoin. This shows why it's essential to always keep yourself abreast of any occurrences in the crypto sphere.

Some factors you should consider before deciding on whether you want to invest in a specific cryptocurrency include:

- The transaction processing speed

- The number of coins currently in circulation

- Is the supply of coins limited or unlimited? If limited, what's the limit?

- The real-world applications of the cryptocurrency

- Real world adoption of the technology

- Background of the founders

- Does the project have any big investors?

How to Buy Your First Coins?

For beginners, the first time buying crypto-coins can be confusing and challenging. Before you can buy your first coins, you need to set up your digital wallet. The complexity of buying cryptocurrencies depends on your country's financial system, though it need not be a complicated process. Some of the methods you can use to pay for crypto-coins include:

Bank transfer

This is a simple but slow way of paying for cryptocurrencies. Simply make a transfer to the seller's account and they will send you your coins the moment they receive the money. Bank transfers take about 1-2 days for the money to reflect in the seller's account, this is the period you have to wait for before you receive your coins.

Credit card

Despite being the most common online payment method for fiat money, it is widely unaccepted by cryptocurrency sellers. This is because with credit card payments, malicious buyers can claim chargebacks, therefore defrauding the seller. Since cryptocurrency transactions are irreversible, the seller would have no way of getting back their coins. Still, some exchanges accept credit card payments, though they charge higher prices for the cryptocurrencies.

PayPal

Just like credit cards, PayPal payments are widely unaccepted by cryptocurrency sellers because of the issue of chargebacks. Some exchanges support PayPal payments, though they also charge significantly higher prices.

Other payment channels

Different exchanges accept many other different payment methods such as Skrill, Sofort, iDEAL and many more.

Private payment channels

You can pay for crypto-coins through other private channels such as Western Union, Paysafecard, or using good old cash. Some p2p platforms like LocalBitcoins link buyers and sellers in the same region, allowing them to decide on their own payment methods.

Once you have figured out the best payment method for you, you can now go ahead and purchase your preferred cryptocurrency. Some common places where you can buy cryptocurrencies include exchange platforms, brokers and direct commercial exchanges, p2p markets like LocalBitcoins, through gift cards and vouchers and from cryptocurrency ATMs.

Cryptocurrency Exchanges

If your intention is to get into cryptocurrency trading, then you will definitely need to join a cryptocurrency exchange. These are platforms that allow users to exchange cryptocurrencies for fiat currencies as well as other cryptocurrencies. There are various kinds of exchanges, each meant to serve a specific kind of user. There are advanced exchanges with complex trading tools to serve professional traders, while others are there to serve people looking to make the occasional trade.

The three main types of exchanges are:

Trading platforms

These connect traders and perform the role of an escrow. They handle the processing of orders and charge fees for each transaction.

Direct trading platforms

Also referred to as p2p markets, these link buyers and sellers directly without playing the role of an intermediary. Instead of having fixed prices, they allow sellers to set their own rates.

Brokers and direct commercial exchanges

These work like FOREX brokers, exchanging cryptocurrencies for other cryptocurrencies and fiat money at fixed prices.

Factors to Consider When Choosing an Exchange

Type the words 'cryptocurrency exchange' into your browser and you'll find several exchanges to choose from. With such a wide pool to choose from, you want to make sure you join a cryptocurrency exchange that best serves your needs. Some factors to keep in mind when choosing a cryptocurrency exchange include:

Reputation

Before joining, find out what other users are saying about the exchange. Read online reviews and scour cryptocurrency communities and forums.

Fees

Cryptocurrency exchanges make money by charging transaction, deposit and withdrawal fees. Find out the fee structure of an exchange before joining to avoid unanticipated charges.

Payment methods

Does the exchange support payment methods that are convenient for you? You should also keep in mind that charges will be higher for exchanges that accept PayPal and credit card payments and that bank transfers are not convenient when you need to make fast transactions.

Verification requirements

Are you looking for complete anonymity? Most exchanges will ask you for identity and proof of address documents before you can start trading. Are you willing to provide this information?

Geographical restrictions

Does the exchange offer full support in your geographic region?

Exchange rates

Cryptocurrency exchanges also make profits from their spreads. Check their rates and spreads to ensure you're getting the best deal.

Evaluating an exchange based on the above considerations will ensure that you join a cryptocurrency exchange that is best suited to your needs. Some popular cryptocurrency exchanges that you might consider include Coinbase, Kraken, Poloniex, Shapeshift and LocalBitcoins.

When Should You Buy?

If you listen to cryptocurrency traders, you will hear them talking about good and bad times to buy. So, when is the best time to buy? There is no rule of the thumb as to when you should buy cryptocurrencies. However, you should avoid buying at the peak of a bubble. Neither should you buy when prices are crashing. As the trader's saying goes, 'Never catch a falling knife'. The best times to buy are when prices are relatively low and stable.

To be a successful trader, you need to learn how to determine when a bubble is about to burst and when the price hits the bottom after falling. That being said, no one can predict this with ultimate certainty. For instance, when Bitcoin rose to $1000, many people were afraid of buying, thinking that this was the peak of the bubble. The price rose to $10000 and many more thought that this must certainly be the peak. Although, Bitcoin defied their prediction and continued rising, nearly hitting the $20000 mark. You should also avoid comparing cryptocurrency bubbles to financial bubbles, since cryptocurrencies are highly volatile.

Risks of Cryptocurrency Investing/Trading

Despite some people having become instant millionaires and billionaires through cryptocurrency investing and trading, this does not mean that there are no risks in it. Here are some risks you face when you decide to become a cryptocurrency investor.

Some technologies will fail

You should keep in mind that cryptocurrencies are basically software or lines of code. Remember the dot.com bust? Some cryptocurrencies will fail in the same way that some software companies failed in the dot.com era. Back in the '90s, there was a lot of hype about the new thing known as the internet, which promised to change the world. Well, the internet did change the world. It created overnight billionaires. But, a lot of people also lost their money there as well. The same thing will happen with cryptocurrency. By investing in a cryptocurrency, you are simply betting on that software. Some will change the world and create immense wealth, while others will fade from the face of the earth. Learn to differentiate winners from losers.

It requires technical savvy

Cryptocurrencies were developed by super-geeks, and to most people, cryptocurrencies are still geeky. To get into cryptocurrency, you need to be good with computers. At least until more user-friendly cryptocurrency interfaces are built. Why am I saying this? With cryptocurrencies, you are dealing with cash. You need to be well-versed with various aspects of computer and internet security. Otherwise, you might wake up to find a zero balance on your digital wallet. You also need to understand the basics of how cryptocurrencies work to enable you to bet on those with the highest chance of success.

Broker and technology risk

Cryptocurrency is still in its infancy, hence there are still lots of unknowns. Many things could change. New security vulnerabilities might emerge. Remember how millions of traders lost their money after the hacking of MtGox? If anything, you should consider dealing with cryptocurrency brokers to be about twice as risky as dealing with FOREX brokers.

Factors That Affect the Price of a Cryptocurrency

Cryptocurrency prices are affected by several factors, sometimes leading to very abrupt changes. Some factors you need to keep in mind include:

Exchange listing

This is a major mover of cryptocurrency prices. Whenever a large cryptocurrency exchange announces that they will start listing a certain cryptocurrency, you can expect the price to shoot soon.

Software upgrades

Cryptocurrencies undergo software upgrades either to solve existing challenges in the network or to improve functionality. For example, there was a hotly debated argument about making a software upgrade to improve Bitcoin's transaction processing speed. This argument ended with the split of Bitcoin Cash from Bitcoin. Watch out for software upgrades since they are highly likely to affect the price of a cryptocurrency.

Public hype

Just like company stocks, cryptocurrency prices can be affected by fake news.

Wallet improvements

Some investors buy cryptocurrencies and hold them for a couple years as they wait for prices to rise. Hence, storage is an important part of the cryptocurrency equation. In their initial stages, most cryptocurrencies are still geeky, with wallets that are not beginner friendly. This keeps the non-techie investors from these cryptocurrencies. Therefore, cryptocurrencies without good wallets are often undervalued. Introduction of a better, user-friendly wallet opens these cryptocurrencies to the masses and therefore often leads to an increase in price.

Platform applications

Some cryptocurrency platforms are more than digital currencies. For instance, Ethereum is a platform that allows the building and deployment of other applications. If one of the applications built on a cryptocurrency platform does well, it can lead to an increase in the value of the underlying platform. Consequently, it's good to watch out for any promising apps that are hosted on the cryptocurrency platform you are trading in.

Government regulation

Government policies also influence the effect of cryptocurrencies. For instance, Bitcoin prices fell before rebounding in September 2017 after China announced that it had banned cryptocurrency trading in the country. You should keep abreast of any government policy trends and avoid cryptocurrencies that are likely to be red flagged by governments.

Cryptocurrency vs. Fiat Currency

Fiat currency, whether in digital or cash, is essentially the currency that is regulated and controlled by the government. Unless you're using that currency, you cannot technically buy anything within that country since it's the "official" money of that country. When purchasing anything in other country using digital means like a credit card, the computer will do the money converting for you, for example as the purchase is made, your US dollars and converting them into British pounds. You're forced to go somewhere else or a bank to get your dollars exchanged for the pounds so that you can then go out and make your purchases, if you only have cash. On the other, cryptocurrency can be used in any country because its value is the same no matter where in the world you are, and it has no such regulations from the government. First advantage of trading with cryptocurrency rather than fiat currency is brought about there.

A lost wallet means that any that you had in the bank is permanently lost, so you have to make a call to cancel your debit or credit and get a new one. Cryptocurrency cannot. In addition, the governments and banks of the world have the right to destroy fiat currency since they are the ones who control and create it. Your money is always safe since nobody can do that to your cryptocurrency.

Trading, selling and buying can take place just in half the time since cryptocurrency also takes just minutes to transfer. Something as simple as transferring money from one person's account to another, can take days especially, during the weekends, since fiat currency needs to pass through a bunch of checkpoints and regulations. Whether it's taxes, from your bank or anything else for transferring money you also do not have to pay a fee. Nothing should worry you about the value of money going down or up. The money's value is international with cryptocurrency since the market is international. No matter when you're trading or where you are or who you're buying from or what you're saying, it'll stay the same. You are assured of your money's value.

This means that you have control over your cryptocurrency. It is you but not a government or a bank. You know how much value it will have down the line and your cryptocurrency's value. You don't have to worry about the money being taxed, taken away, destroyed, by the government or banks and you know how much you spend. Within minutes, you receive and give money quickly. Rather than finding yourself at the mercy of institutions that don't care and are not controlled and regulated the way that they should, you can manage your finances. You also do not have to report anything to anyone. Your bank can stop a transfer of funds if it seems suspicious to them and is always in control of where you spend your money. You do not have any privacy as always have to be able to explain your funds and how they are spent. You do not have someone breathing down your neck that way with cryptocurrency. You do not need to worry about having your account frozen because while vacationing in Europe you bought a computer, since you have privacy all is well with you.

Taxes

People are forced every year to pay their large sums of money to government, and often those who can least afford to pay are the ones paying the most. When the poor are already struggling with the bills, they have to hand over money while the rich hardly get anything taken away. You don't have to worry about anything that you own being taken away from you with cryptocurrency. Unless you want to, you don't have to report to the government tax agency since cryptocurrency is untaxed. What you do with your currency is not the government, but it's up to you because cryptocurrency recognizes your sovereignty.

Therefore, cryptocurrency holds less advantage compared to fiat currency, that is the legal issue. Some governments try to regulate cryptocurrency, such as the United States which categorizes cryptocurrency as property rather than income, and subject to a property tax if you report it, while others forbid cryptocurrency. You might want to ensure that you're at least familiar with the law in regard to cryptocurrency or that you're careful about the law depending on the country you come from.

Note that this might be something that makes you unsure about cryptocurrency. The reason governments are having such a problem with it is that they cannot regulate it. When you cannot properly explain why the thing someone was doing is wrong, it's hard to bring the law down on them. The governments cannot take people to task for using cryptocurrencies until they come up with solid rules for it. You are being busted probably in the cryptocurrency community as well if you're getting busted by the government for using cryptocurrency, there are exceptions.

Inflation

Inflation is where the cash out in the world is higher in amount, resulting it to be less valuable. Where there is more of something it is less valuable. It means that your bill of one dollar has less value since you'll be able to buy less from it, and so to make up the difference, suppliers are asking for more money. There is a cap in the cryptocurrency world on how many cryptocurrencies are there. For instance, bitcoin has a cap of 21 million bitcoins. A "controlled supply" was created by this and its value is assured since it's finite and controlled. As new coins are created so that there is not more than the cap out in circulation, they are designed to eventually go out of circulation.

This makes sure that the value of your cryptocurrency won't collapse suddenly and that there is no inflation. There is security unlike with fiat money. The value of your bitcoin will rise over time, something that occurs with gemstones and metal but not with fiat money.

Trading vs. Buying

The terms **trading** and **buying** are often used synonymously. However, for the word geeks out there, there are certain differences between the two. On the one hand, when you **buy** cryptocurrencies, it involves actually buying cryptocurrencies. To make a profit, then you need to engage in a buy and sell activity, which is merely about buying low and selling high via an exchange platform. When you do this, you offer your cryptocurrencies at full value when you open a position. On the other hand, when you **trade** cryptocurrencies, you make a speculation when a particular market will rise or fall. Take note that unlike buying cryptocurrencies, you do not take ownership of the cryptocurrencies that you trade, but you merely speculate as to their price movements. Trading also usually involves what is known as margin trading. Margin trading is like the FOREX where you can leverage your position by borrowing cryptocurrencies from your trading broker. This way you can trade with much bigger funds even if you don't really have a well-funded trading account. Needless to say, this will allow you to earn a really high amount of profit even if you only invested a small capital. However, this approach is not advisable for beginners as it can be costly in the long run since you'll have to pay interest to your trading broker.

Understanding high volatility

The cryptocurrency market is known for having high volatility. But, what does **high volatility** really mean? When you say that the cryptocurrency market has a high volatility, it means that the price of the cryptocurrencies fluctuates rapidly and significantly. To give you an example, there was a time when the price of bitcoin increases by $2,000 in just a few days, but there was also an incident when its price dropped also by $2,000 just as fast. It should also be noted that high volatility is not something that balances itself out in the long run. A common misconception of high volatility is that after a significant increase in price, then it would be followed by a significant decrease in price, and vice versa. But this is not always the case. It's possible for an increase in price to be followed by another increase or even a series of increases. In the same way, a drop-in price and still be followed by another significant decrease or even a series of decreases. Of course, the rise and fall of the price of a cryptocurrency can also happen in a seemingly random manner. The point here is that the cryptocurrency market does not balance itself out unless there are factors that will move the price of a cryptocurrency to do so. This means that cryptocurrencies don't move at random but are influenced by numerous factors and elements, such as the economy, the competition among the different cryptocurrencies, market acceptance, the news, and other technological developments, among other things.

Chapter 2: Risk Management Techniques in Day Trading

Understanding Risk

Risk is at the heart of all types of investment as without it there would be no need for a reward. As such, options trading is risky at the best of times, even for those considered experts and certainly for those still new to the field. Luckily, there are ways to mitigate that risk since many of the major pitfalls of options trading have been well documented by those who have come before. What's more, they have also been distilled down and classified so that all you need to do is memorize the following and ensure that you do your best to not let it intrude on your trading success.

It does not matter what type of trade you're working with, the first thing you're going to want to do is to take three main things into consideration. First, you will want to be aware of how much a specific price is likely going to change prior to the expiration of the option in question. From there, you will want to determine how volatile the underlying asset is as well as how much time the option has, to turn you a profit prior to its expiration. When you're purchasing options, it's important to also identify the direction you expect the underlying stock to move in as well as how long you expect it to continue to move in the specified direction. In these instances, the amount of time that is available won't be as significant when it comes to ensuring the overall maximum value.

To minimize risk efficiently, you should know that the best strategies focus on either high positive or high negative risk value, there is little value in betting on the middle ground. Remember, some option types are always going to end up being more profitable than others in specific scenarios, you just need to have the patience and the foresight to know what is coming before it gets here. With that being said, you should always keep in mind that statistical projections cannot predict the future because any analysis that is done is strictly hypothetical. Never invest more money into a trade, no matter how reliable it seems, than you can ultimately afford to lose.

Manage Market Risk

When people think of day trading, they only think of potential profits, not losses. Thus, day trading attracts so many people, they don't see the risk of losses. In stock markets, various events can trigger losses for investors and traders, which are beyond their control. These events can be economic conditions such as recession, geopolitical changes, changes in the central bank policies, natural disasters, or sometimes terror attacks.

This is the market risk; the potential of losing money due to abrupt unknown factors. These factors affect the overall performance of stock markets, and regardless of how careful one is while day trading, the possibility of market risk is always present, which can cause losses. The market risk is known as the systematic risk because it influences the entire stock market. There is also a nonsystematic risk, which affects only a specific industry or company. Long-term investors tackle this risk by diversification in their investment portfolio.

Unlike investors, day traders have no method to neutralize market risk, but they can avoid it by keeping track of financial and business events, news, and economic calendars. For example, stock markets are very sensitive to the central banks' rate policies and become highly volatile on those days. Nobody knows what kind of policy any central bank will adopt in its monetary meeting. But day traders can check the economic calendar and know which day these meetings will take place. They can avoid trading on those days and reduce the risk of loss in trading.

Therefore, knowledge of stock markets and being aware of what is happening in the financial world is essential for day traders. Many successful traders have a policy of staying away from trading on days where a major economic event takes place, or a decision is announced. For example, on the day when the result of an impactful election is declared; any big company's court case decision comes in, or a central banks' policy meeting takes place. On such days, speculative trading dominates stock markets and market risk is very high. Similarly, on a day when any company announces earnings results, its stock price fluctuates wildly, increasing the market risk in trading of that stock.

For inexperienced day traders, the best way to tackle market risk is to avoid trading on such days.

Using Risk-Reward Ratio

Day trading is done for financial rewards and the good thing is, you can always calculate how much risk you take on every trade and how much reward you can expect. The risk-reward ratio represents the expected reward and expected risk traders can earn on the investment of every dollar.

The risk-reward ratio can quiet clearly indicate your potential profits and potential loss, which can help you in managing your investment capital. For example, a trade with the risk-reward ratio of 1:4 shows that at the risk of $1, the trade has the potential of returning $4. Professional traders advise not to take any trade which has a risk-reward ratio lower than 1:3. This indicates, the trader can expect the investment to be $1, and the potential profit $3.

Expert traders use this method for planning which trade will be more profitable and take only those trades. Technical charting is a good technique to decide the risk-reward ratio of any trade by plotting the price moment from support to resistance levels. For example, if a stock has a support level at $20, it'll probably rise from that level because many traders are likely to buy it at support levels. After finding out a potential support level, traders try to spot the nearby resistance level where the rising price is expected to pause. Suppose a technical level is appearing at $60. So, the trader can buy at $20 and exit when the price reaches $60. If everything goes right, he can risk $20 to reap a reward of $60. In this trade, the risk-reward ratio will be 1:3.

By calculating the risk-reward ratio, traders can plan how much money they will need to invest, and how much reward they can expect to gain from any trade. This makes them cautious about money and risk management.

Some traders have a flexible risk-reward ratio for trading, while others prefer to take trades only with a fixed risk-reward ratio. Keeping stop-loss in all trades also helps in managing the risk-reward ratio. Traders can calculate their trade entry point to stop-loss as the risk, and trade entry to profit as the reward. This way, they can find out if any trade has a bigger risk than the potential reward or a bigger reward than the potential risk. Choosing trades with bigger profits and smaller risks can increase the amount of profit over a period.

Without learning money management, all your knowledge about stock and day trading is useless. If you don't use effective techniques for managing your investment, then you may soon find your money running out and you'll have to shut down your day trading business. There are various methods for money management in intraday trading. It will be a good idea to learn a few techniques for it and it and strictly apply those rules to your trading business. Keeping the trading cost to a minimum and putting stop-loss in all trades are effective money management tricks.

Margin trading facilities are given for day trading and can be used astutely for increasing profits. At the same time, margin facilities can make day traders greedy, make them commit the mistake of over-trading, and incurring losses. Margin facility is borrowing money from your brokerage firm and trading on borrowed money is never a good idea. It's better to avoid margin trading until you have enough experience in stock markets and can handle your emotions while trading.

Day trading is not only profitable but can always lead to losses because of the ever-present market risk. Various events can trigger this risk and affect the performance of the overall stock markets. Day traders have no control over it. Still, many strategies can help day traders avoid market risk, and reduce the potential loss that it can cause. Knowledge of stock markets' functioning and checking economic calendars can help day traders avoid some market risks.

Traders always face the risk of financial loss. So, they must use strategies for risk management in day trading. Protecting your trading capital should be your first aim so you can stay in the day trading business for the long term. Creating trading plans and trading strategies are steps that can help traders avoid loss-making trades. Using stop orders is another method that can help traders reduce the losses and book their profits at the right time.

Calculating the risk-reward ratio is another method for money management and risk reduction. Traders can calculate how much risk a trade carries and how much potential profit it can earn for them. They can choose only those trades that carry a bigger reward and smaller risk and thus earn more profits in the long-term. Some professional traders prefer to trade only when the rewards are much higher than the potential risk.

Chapter 3: Technical Indicators to Build A Trading Toolkit

On-Balance Volume

First up, utilize the on-balance volume marker (OBV) to quantify the positive and negative progression of volume in security after some time. The tag is a running aggregate of up volume short down volume. Up volume is how much volume there is on the day when the cost mobilized. Downsize is the volume on a day when the value falls. Daily volume is included or subtracted from the marker dependent on whether the price went sequential.

When OBV is rising, it shows that purchasers are eager to step in and push the cost higher. When OBV falls, the selling volume is outpacing purchasing volume, which shows lower prices. Right now, it acts as a pattern   affirmation device. On the off

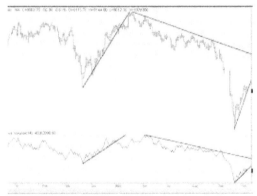

chance that cost and OBV are rising, that shows a continuation of the pattern.

Brokers who use OBV additionally watch for dissimilarity. This happens when the pointer and cost are veering off. So, if the the price is rising; but OBV is falling, it means the pattern isn't upheld by solid purchasers and could before the long opposite.

Collection/Distribution Line

One of the most ordinarily utilized markers to decide the cash stream all through security is the gathering/circulation line (A/D line). It is like the on-balance volume marker (OBV). Yet, as opposed to considering just the end cost of the security for the period, it likewise considers the trading range for the period and where the nearby is corresponding to that extend. If a stock completes close to its high, the marker gives volume more weight than if it closes close to the midpoint of its range. The various computations imply that OBV will work better at times, and A/D will work better in others.

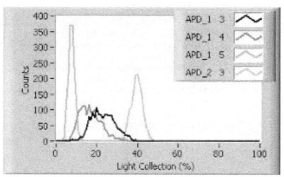

If the pointer line is slanting up, it shows purchasing enthusiasm, since the stock is shutting over the midpoint of the range. This affirms an upturn. Then again, if A/D is falling, that implies the cost is completing in the lower bit of its everyday range, and hence volume is viewed as unfavorable. This affirms a downtrend.

Brokers utilizing the A/D line additionally watch for the disparity. If the A/D begins falling while the cost is rising, this signals the pattern is in a tough situation and could turn around. Thus, if the price is drifting lower and A/D begins rising, that could flag more significant expenses to come.

Normal Directional Index

The standard directional file (ADX) is a pattern marker used to gauge the quality and force of a pattern. At the point when the ADX is over 40, the design is considered to have a lot of directional quality, either up or down, contingent upon the bearing the cost is moving. At the point when the ADX pointer is underneath 20, the pattern is viewed as powerless or non-inclining. The ADX is the primary line on the marker,

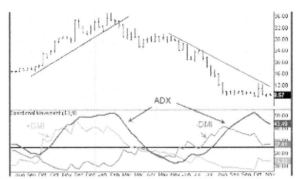

generally hued dark. Two extra lines can alternatively appear. These are DI+ and DI-. These lines are regularly shaded red and green, individually. Every one of the three lines cooperates to show the heading of the pattern just as the force of the design.

ADX over 20 and DI+ above DI-: That's an upturn.

ADX over 20 and DI-above DI+: That's a downtrend.

ADX underneath 20 is a feeble pattern or running period, frequently connected with the DI-and DI+ quickly jumbling one another.

MACD

The Moving Normal Union Dissimilarity (MACD) marker assists traders with seeing the pattern heading, just as the energy of that pattern. It likewise gives various exchange signals. At the point when the MACD is over zero, the cost is in an upward stage. If the MACD is underneath zero, it has entered a bearish period.

39

So, the MACD, in that case, would be crossing beneath the signing line and this may give the sign to flag a potential short exchange.

Relative Strength Index

The comparative quality list (RSI) has, in any event, three significant employments. The pointer moves somewhere in the range of zero and 100, plotting late value gains versus ongoing value misfortunes. The RSI levels along these lines help in measuring energy and pattern quality.

The essential utilization of an RSI is an overbought and oversold market. When RSI moves over 70, the benefit is considered overbought and could decrease. At the point when the RSI is underneath 30, the interest is oversold and could mobilize. Notwithstanding, making this risky supposition; along these lines, a few traders trust that the marker will transcend 70 and afterward dip under before selling, or dip under 30 and eventually ascend back above before purchasing.

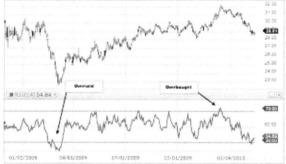

The disparity is another utilization of the RSI. At the point when the pointer is moving an unexpected way in comparison to the value, it shows that the present value pattern is debilitating and could before long converse. A third use for the RSI is backing and obstruction levels. During upturns, a stock will regularly hold over the 30 degrees, and now and again, arrive at 70 or above. At the point when a stock is in a downtrend, the RSI will ordinarily hold underneath 70, and now and again arrive at 30 or beneath.

Stochastic Oscillator

The stochastic oscillator is a marker that quantifies the present value comparative with the value run over various periods. Plotted somewhere in the range of zero and 100, the thought is that, when the pattern is up, the cost ought to make new highs. In a downtrend, the value tends to make new lows. The stochastic tracks whether this is happening.

The stochastic goes here and there generally rapidly as it is uncommon at the cost to make constant highs, keeping the stochastic close to, 100 or persistent lows, keeping the stochastic almost zero. Hence, the stochastic is frequently utilized as an overbought and oversold pointer. Qualities over 80 are considered overbought, while levels

beneath 20 are considered oversold.

Consider the general value pattern when utilizing overbought and oversold levels. For instance, during an upturn, when the pointer dips under 20 and transcends it, that is a conceivable purchase signal. However, rallies over 80 are less considerable since we hope to see the pointer to move to 80 or more routinely during an upturn. During a downtrend, search for the marker to drive over 80 and afterward drop back beneath to flag a potential short exchange. The 20 level is less massive in a downtrend.

Chapter 12: Day Trading Strategy Basics

Anyone who wishes to make money with the stock trading should have a better strategy on how to predict the trend in prices of the stock in order to maximize profits. The charts show trends that have different patterns a beginner cannot easily interpret. The patterns in the trend have meanings that give signals to the trader on when to make a move by either buying or selling stock. These patterns are discussed below in details.

The ABCD Pattern

This is a harmonic pattern that is used to derive the other patterns of trade. This pattern is made up of three swings that are made up of the AB and CD lines, also known as the legs. The line BC is known as the correction line. The lines AB and CD are almost of the same size. The AB-CD pattern uses a downtrend that indicates that the reversal will be upward. On the other hand, the bearish pattern uses the uptrend than indicates there will be a reversal downward at some point. When using this pattern for trade, you must know the direction of the trend and the movement of the market. There are three types of ABCD pattern: the classic ABCD pattern, the AB=CD pattern, and the ABCD extension.

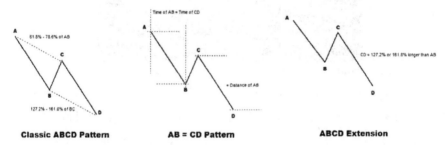

Classic ABCD Pattern   **AB = CD Pattern**   **ABCD Extension**

When using this pattern, remember that one can only enter the trade when the price has reached point D. Hence, it is crucial to study the chart o at the lows and highs; you can use the zigzag indicator, which marks the swings on the chart. As you study the chart, watch the price that forms AB and BC. In a bullish trade ABCD, C should be at the lower side of A. The point A, on the other hand, should be intermediate-high after B that is at a low point. D should be a new point that is lower than B. as mentioned earlier, the entry is at point D, but when the market reaches point D, you should not be too quick to enter the trade, consider other techniques that would make sure that the reverse is up when it's a bullish trade, and down when it's a bearish trade.

Red-to-Green Trading

Every day, stocks are traded, and each day has its own opening and closing price of a certain stock. When the price of the stock for the day is lower than the closing price of the previous day, the trade is considered red. Conversely, when it is trading at a price that is higher than the closing price, the trade is considered green. The two cases represent an opportunity of trading, depending on whether it's bullish or bearish. When the trade is bullish, the trade should make a move to trade when the trading price of the stock is higher than the previous day's closing price. However, when the trade is

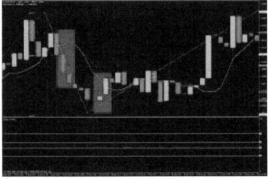

bearish, the trade should only make a move when the trading price of the stock is lower than the closing price of the previous day. These changes in price indicate an important shift in the trading chart, and it can easily be used to plan for trades and make profits. This strategy is perfect if used at the opening time of the trading day when the market is still dynamic. For those who do significant trades during the day, this strategy is good as it provides intraday trading setups.

After Hours Trading

The equities markets in the United States usually close down at 4.00 pm eastern time. Even then, traders continue to have access to the markets until 8.00 pm in the night. Access is enabled via platforms such as ECN and exchanges such as the NYSE. Therefore, trading the markets any time after 4.00 pm till 8.00 pm in the night is referred to as after-hours trading, post-market trading, or extended hours trading. The problem with this trading period is that it's very illiquid as most trading specialists and market makers avoid trading at these times.

The most outstanding feature of after-hours trading is the lack of liquidity in the market.

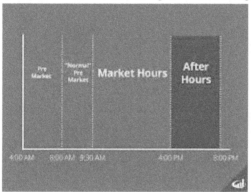

A lot of experts consider this to be risky or even dangerous territory because there is often very little activity. Spreads are often very wide as most of the other traders, especially market makers, have left for the day. Consequently, the securities' activity is often very low. Still, day traders know how to benefit from such situations. For instance, if breaking news is announced during this period, then related stocks could have significant action that can be traded.

Trading after hours is tricky due to the illiquid nature of most securities as well as the large spreads. The best time to trade after hours is only when there is a significant news item that affects a company or industry. Such news is best if received during the earnings periods, which occur mostly during quarterly earnings reporting times. This kind of trading should, therefore, be left to seasoned traders only.

Range Trading

Range trading is often compared to trend following; however, they are different techniques. When you use range trading, you will watch a stock over a certain period. Like other techniques, the increase and decline of prices will present a pattern which is noticeable to the trader. The trader will watch the prices until they see a breakout in the pattern. A breakout is when the price dramatically inflates. The opposite of this, a breakdown, is when the price dramatically declines from its pattern. Once this happens, traders feel that this pattern will continue for some time.

In order to reduce risks when it comes to this strategy, traders will often set high and low limits. This means that once they have viewed where the stock's pattern is sitting for a couple of hours, they will set the highest and lowest price they will buy or sell. Then, once the breakout or breakdown occurs, the trader will proceed with buying or selling the stock.

Momentum Trading

Day traders choose momentum trading simply because all the action is on the stock market momentum. This type of day trading aims at profiting from stocks that experience a price gain, especially with huge trade volumes. In momentum trading, stocks and securities are affected by factors such as margin calls, short squeezes, and stop-losses, so they move in an excessive and extreme manner. The typical approach

by day traders on momentum trading is to scalp profits as quickly as possible and with as much leverage as possible.

Day traders who prefer momentum trading usually trade any security that has large volatility and significant volume. These include securities that have sustained a significant rise in price and are known as high-flyers or momentum stocks. Most of the stocks suitable for this kind of trade strategy are more volatile than those of major blue-chip companies. It is this volatility that attracts momentum traders to these trades. Volatility provides a great option to benefit from price movements and volume. Securities with large volumes and high volatility that feature in the news are usually the best suited to momentum trading.

Price movement: This is the hallmark of momentum day trading. Traders often make use of shorter time frame charts like the 15-minute, 5-minute, and even the 1-minute charts. In order to manage risk, the focus should be on the immediate action with large share volumes. It is principal for momentum day traders to have precision when entering and leaving the market.

Executions and charts will, in this case, carry significantly more weight compared to the fundamentals of the underlying company. Also, stories in the news carry more weight as news is often the main driver of momentum. In addition, chart patterns and essential signals will help determine the best times to initiate trades.

Things momentum traders should look out for

•High probability chart patterns

46

•Intraday setups

•Volume

•The reasonable risk to reward ratios

Options Day Trading

A stock option is yet another trading option commonly used by day traders. Options contracts ideally offer the holder a right with no obligation to sell or purchase an underlying security at a certain price. Options are actually derivatives. This means that their price is derived from an underlying security or even commodity. Therefore, like other derivatives, stock options enable the holder to enjoy the benefits of the price movement of the underlying security, yet the losses they can incur are capped on the option.

A stock options trader basically enjoys the benefits of stock ownership without the obligation or financial implication of having to buy the stock. They only incur costs that are a fraction of the total cost of buying or investing in the stock. Each and every options contract has about 100 shares of the underlying security attached to it. So, a trader holding 10 call or put options basically has control of 1000 shares of the underlying stock.

Many exchanges accept and trade in options contracts. These include exchanges such as the International Securities Exchange, Chicago Boards Options, and many others. This is also since their prices move up and down in tandem with the underlying stock. Although, options are unlike stocks because they can lose most of their value should their time expire. All options have an expiry date as an inherent aspect.

Penny Stocks Trading

What are penny stocks? These are stocks trading on the markets that are worth less than $5 each. They constitute some of the most speculative shares in the market, and most of the times are priced at less than $3 and even $1. There is always the concern about fraud, speculation, and even pump and dump tendencies. However, things have improved, and so penny stocks are now viewed as a less expensive option for investing in stocks at the markets.

The essential ingredients when trading penny stocks are volumes and liquidity. These two ingredients make it easy to enter and exit trades. It is also essential that any day

trader dealing in penny stocks have direct access to a brokerage to execute any trades fast and seamlessly. Penny stocks have a tendency of increased volumes then peaking eventually and leaving plenty of traders trapped with expensive shares. Before entering such trades, it's essential to perform exhaustive research and make use of all tools and leverage in order to have the best information you can. With penny stocks, the essential point to remember is that price is key so always have an exit plan way before commencing any trade.

Pre-market Trading

Another type of day trading strategy is pre-market trading. Trading in these markets begins as early as 4.00 am EST even though the normal pre-market trading hours start at 8.00 am EST. It is during the normal trading hours that liquidity and high volumes begin to stream in. regular trading starts at 09.30 am EST.

Pre-market trading is generally accessible via dark pools and ECNs. This is very similar to after-hours trading. While there are generally no specialists or market makers in the market at such hours, it's probable that they're participating in the markets via certain ECNs.

Reversal Trading

Reversal trading, also known as a trend reversal pattern, is a trading strategy that indicates the end of a trend and the start of a new one. This pattern is formed when the price level of stock in the current trend has reached a maximum. This pattern provides information on the possible change of trend and potential value of price movement. A pattern that is formed in the upwards trend signals that there would be a reversal in the trend, with the prices going down soon. Conversely, a downward trend will indicate that there will be an upward movement of the prices. For you to recognize this pattern, you have to know where specific patterns form in the current trend. There are distribution patterns that occur at the top of the market; at this point, traders sell more than they buy. The patterns that occur at the bottom of the markets are referred to as accumulation patterns, and at this point, traders buy more than they sell.

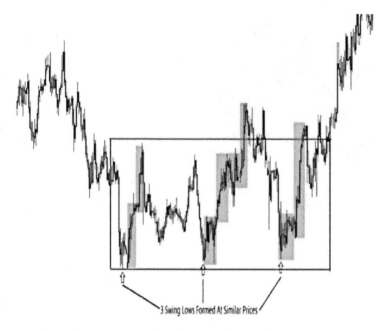

3 Swing Lows Formed At Similar Prices

Reversal

trends are formed at all time frames, and it's because the bank traders have either place trades are taking profits off the trades. The trend can be detected when there are multiple up and down formations that are fully formed; they should be at least two upswings and two downswings indicating a bearish pattern. The swing highs of lows on the trend line depend on which reversal pattern is formed.

The highs or lows form at a similar price because the bank traders want to appear as if they are causing a reversal in the market, by getting all their trades places at the same time. In the real sense that is not the case because they appear at different points of the trend. So, as a trader, you should wait for a clear and steady trend upward for you to sell in the case of a bullish trade and a steady trend downward for the case of a bearish trade for you to buy.

There are different types of reversal patterns. The double top reversal pattern is a pattern that has two tops on the chart. It looks like "M." The double top has its reverse type known as the double bottom pattern that resembles "W." The double bottom has two bottoms located either on the same support or at different supports.

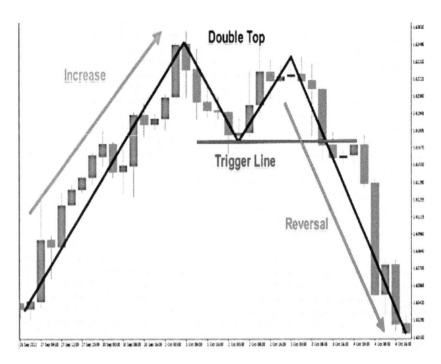

Another reversal pattern is the head and shoulders; this pattern resembled two shoulders and ahead. The two shoulders are tops that are slightly below the other top that is known as the head. The head and shoulders can also be represented in a descending pattern whereby the tops become bottoms.

Volume Weighted Average Price (VWAP) Trading

VWAP trading takes the price and volume of a stock to give you an average price. It is known as a trading benchmark and will give traders an idea of the trend and security of the stock. Like most trading strategies, the VWAP can be used with specific software that will perform the algorithms for each step. However, it's possible to calculate the VWAP yourself.

This type of strategy can be used by various investors and traders. For example, both day traders and buy-and-hold investor s can use the VWAP technique. Though, it is more popular with short-term trades. This strategy will start new at the beginning of the day and give you a running total at the end of the day. This is one of the reasons buy-and-hold investors use this strategy, as it allows them to analyze the stock.

Electronic Communication Network (ECN) and Level II

This type of strategy involves watching the trades in real time. It's like going to a horse race and watching the race to see if you're going to win or lose your money. The ECN is an automated system where traders from all over can trade with you. Day traders who take on the business by themselves, without the help of a broker, usually use the ECN strategy because it's fairly easy to navigate and is known to take out any middleman. This is a benefit as it takes away any brokerage fees and can make trades more profitable because it's known to save time. On top of this, the ECN allows for after-market trading, which means you can trade after the regular trading hours of the day.

There are several charts available that will allow you to see the price changes of stocks throughout the day. All the charts will allow you to compare the opening price to the closing price. On top of this, the charts show you the various price changes in the stock during the day.

Spread Trading

Spread trading, also known as scalping, is defined as trading securities over a period of seconds to minutes. The reason this type of technique has become popular is because traders feel that they can catch stocks easier when they follow small growths over large

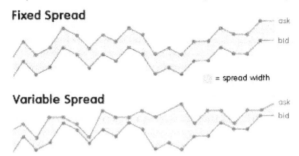

increments. The number of transactions day traders go through can vary from a dozen to over 200 within a day. Traders make so many transactions because they will sell the stock as soon as it gives them a profit.

This type of technique is known to be relatively safe, which is another reason why so many traders consider themselves spread traders. Traders who follow this technique are often considered to be market makers, as they help maintain the liquidity of the market.

If you are thinking about looking more into this strategy, then you should note the following three points:

Low Profits Comes from Large Volume

Traders who use the spread trading technique state this strategy is not useful for people who want to move large volumes of shares at one time. They won't be able to make the money they want by using this strategy as large volumes give low profits. This happens because the profit margin, which is the measure of profitability, neglects the large volume investor. This is why, the best type of traders for spread trading are the ones who are interested in moving small volumes.

You Will Have a Lower Risk if You Lower Your Exposure

Traders who take on the technique of scalping will limit their risk of loss because they don't hang onto their stocks for a long period of time. In fact, most traders will hold on to the majority of their shares for only a few minutes, very rarely reaching an hour.

Smaller Moves are Easier

People who follow this technique become pros at finding the small moves with the small spreads that tend to happen frequently throughout the day. The reason spread traders focus on small moves is not only because they are easier to handle using this technique but also because this is where they find their best profits.

Trend Following

Traders refer to trend following as trading stocks because of their affinity to trends over their market value. This type of technique is not only used in day trading, but in all types of stock market transactions. How long you will follow the trend before you decide to take a stock because of its trend depends on what type of trading you're doing. In day trading, you won't spend more than a couple of hours on the trend. However, if you're into swing trading, you might analyze the trend for a few days to a couple of weeks.

Many traders like to take part in this technique because they feel that they know what

the stock is going to do. Because you have watched for a trend to develop and then analyzed the trend to make sure it's a purchase you would like to make, your confidence about what the stock will do in the future increases. On top of this, many traders feel that they are more likely to succeed in making a profit because they can watch for stocks that will give you capital instead of loss.

At the same time, you always want to pay attention to all the factors that affect the trend of a stock. The factors you should consider if you decide to use trend following are:

Fading

Not a lot of traders take part in fading because it's known to be one of the riskier strategies. Unless you have a good amount of experience in trading, it is best that you don't participate in fading, as it is considered a more advanced technique in the business. The basis of short selling is that the trader speculates on the stock's decline. Speculation means that the trader makes the transaction when the risk of losing capital is high because the trader expects that there will be a benefit or some type of gain from the trade.

Fading doesn't follow the trends of the market. They buy when the price of the stock is low and sell when the price is high. They often buy a stock when they feel the market has overreacted over recent news. One of the benefits is that there is little analysis that needs to be done before buying or selling.

Stop-Loss Trading

This type of strategy involves making a deal with your broker to sell a stock once it reaches a certain price. This is a popular strategy, in fact most experienced traders say you should use stop-loss trading because it gives you security in your business. This happens because you can decide to say that you'll sell the stock when it is 13% below your purchasing price.

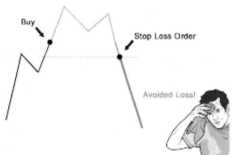

This type of strategy isn't always used to for day trading because sometimes the stock won't reach the percentage you set. Therefore, you continue to hold the stock and don't sell it at the end of the day.

Flag Momentum

In a trading market, there are times when things are good and the traders enjoy an upward trend, which gives a chart pattern that represents a bull flag pattern. It is named as such because when you look at the chart, it forms a pattern that resembles a flag on a pole. The trend in the market is an uptrend, and the pattern is then referred to as a bullish flag. The bull flag pattern is characterized by the following; when the stock makes a positive move with a relatively high volume, the pole is formed, when the stock consolidates on a lighter volume at the top, the flag is formed. The stock continues to move at a relatively high volume breaking through the consolidation pattern. This is a trading strategy that can be used at any given time frame. When it's used to scalp the movements of price, the bull is used only on two instances of time frame: the second and the fifth minute time frames. It also works well when using daily charts to trade and can also be used effectively when swing trading.

It is simple to trade, but it is challenging to look for the exact bull pattern. This problem can be solved using scanners that help to look for stocks on the upward trend and wait for them to be in a consolidation position at the top. The best and free scanners that can be used to locate bull flags are FINVIZ and ChartMill. There are tips that can be used to indicate a bull flag. When there is an increase in stock volume that is influenced by news, and when the stock prices remain high, showing a clear pattern for a pullback. At this point, you can now check out when the prices break out above the consolidation pattern or on high volumes of stock. To make a move, place a stop order at the bottom of the consolidation. At this point, the ratio of risk to reward is 2:1, and it's the best time to target. The strongest part of the pattern is the volume of the stock, and it's a good sign that there will be a major move and a successful breakout. On the trend, it's also good to look at the descending trend as it gives a sign on the next breakout. This can be seen in the trend line that is found on at the top of the flag.

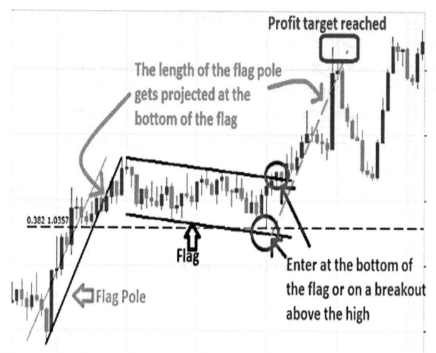

When used well for trading, the bull flags are effective tools of the trade; but things can go wrong, and therefore one must be ready with an exit strategy. There are two strategies, one is placing a stop order at a point below the consolidation area, and the second method is using a moving average that is monitored for within 20 days. Within the 20 days, if the price of the stock is below the moving average, then it's time to close out the position and try out other trading routes.

Moving Average Trend Trading

This strategy of trading is common among traders and it uses technical indicators. A moving average helps to know which way the price is moving, if the moving average is inclined upwards, then the price is moving up, and if it's inclined downwards, then the price is going downwards. Moving average can also help to show resistance or support of the trend, but this depends on the amount of time of the moving average. Support is shown when the trend of the price is downward, and at this point, the selling pressure reduces, and buyers start to step in the market. Resistance is shown when the trend in the price of the stock is upward. At this point, buying of stock reduces and sellers step in. it should be noted that the prices of trade stock don't always follow the moving average, but it's good to know that when the stock price is above the moving average of the trend, then the price trend is upward. Conversely, if the price is below the moving average, then the trend of the price of the stock is downwards.

Moving average is a powerful tool of the trade as it's easy to calculate, which makes it popular among traders. This tool of trade enables the trader to understand the current trend and identify any signs of a reversal. It also helps the trader to determine entry into the trade or an exit, depending on whether it offers support or resistance.

There are different types of moving averages. The simple moving average, which sums up five recent closing prices and calculates the average price, another one is the exponential moving average, whose calculation is a bit complex because it applies more weighting to the data that is most recent. When the simple moving average and the exponential moving averages are compared, the exponential moving average is affected more by the changes in prices than the simple moving average.

High-Frequency Trading

High-frequency trading, also referred to as HFT, are essentially programs that execute complex algorithms that can generate superfast trades across different markets. The purpose of these rapid trades includes arbitrage and market making. The outstanding feature here is the thin profits that accrue from the large volumes of trades initiated. Trades initiated can number in their millions on any given day. It is said that about 50% or half of the volume trades initiated in US stock markets are HFT.

These trades rarely hold a position for long. One of the most useful ingredients in any HFT operation is low latency in order to keep the speed advantage over other traders such as retail traders. It is a modern computer algorithm that power HFTs. If well executed, such programs can generate modest to average profits for a long period of time without incurring any significant losses. There are reports of HFT firms of running for 1000 profitable days without any losses. When everything works as required, it offers a great opportunity to earn plenty of money with very little risk over a long period of time.

Latency: This term refers to the time taken for data transmitted between two points to get to its destination. Basically, low latency refers to high speeds, while high means low speeds. Most investment companies invest a lot of resources in acquiring the latest, cutting edge infrastructure and hardware necessary for processing trades at high speeds.

Algorithms: These are basically instructions set out which are to be executed once certain conditions are met. A sophisticated algorithm such as the HFC algorithm used in trade has millions of lines of code. In recent years, algorithms have become commonplace, and most traders make use of one type or another to execute their trades.

Support or Resistance Trading

As traders buy and sell their stock, there are changes in the price of the stock being exchanged, and this depends on the supply and demand of a stock. As trade continues, there are instances where there is support or resistance in the market. Support is when the price of the stock tends to stabilize or stop falling, while resistance is when the price of the stock tends to stabilize at a point and stop to rise. These two occurrences can be used in trading; however, one must understand the trend of the trade first. Support is a level of price of the stock where the demand of the stock is strong and thus prevents downward movement of the price. As the price of the stock gets near the support, the prices lower and the buyers consider it easier to buy. This reduces the number of sellers because they don't have a good deal for their stock. In this case, because the demand for the stock surpasses the supply, the price of the stock is prevented from falling below the support.

Resistance presents a case in the market that the supply is strong to control the rise of the price of the stock. In this case, as the stock price gets close to the resistance level, the price of the stock increases, making them expensive. This makes the buyers step back, and supply overcomes demand and therefore controls the rise in the price of the stock. There are four strategies that can be used to trade using support and resistance. The first one is using range trading, which takes place in the region between the resistance and support. In this region, buyers are trying to buy, and the sellers are trying to sell. To apply this strategy, traders need to establish support and resistance on the trading chart.

61

The price does not always remain within the boundaries of support and resistance, and this can be risky to the traders. Accordingly, to minimize losses, it's always good to set stops that are below the support when the price bounce is long and above the resistance when the bounce is short.

Another strategy is the breakout strategy. When the trade is within the region of uncertainty, there is a possibility that it will move from this region and start to trend. The point at which it starts trending is the breakout point, and all traders are always waiting for this point to maximize the change in trend. This strategy can make a good deal, but sometimes it can cause huge losses due to false breakout. So, it's better to wait before committing to any trade. Trend line strategy is by drawing a line connecting many highs in the downward trend and lows in the upward trend; the trader operates along the line when he wants to buy or sell.

Opening Range Breakouts

The opening time of trading is a good time to make money from your trades if you have a good plan. At this time, the market is dynamic and more active. The opening range breakdown uses reversals of the opening hour to make profits or buy at lower prices. After the market opens, it experiences highs and lows for a given period; this is the time to determine how high the stock will be during the day as well as how low in order to know the range of trading. Traders use this period to predict the price action during the day and set their entry point in the market. A trader that starts to monitor the market from the time of opening is likely to notice an opportunity and maximize it. This strategy is good for full-time traders.

Before trading, one should first measure the opening range in terms of its size, and to do that you look at two candles, the last candle from yesterday's trading and the first candle that was created after the opening of the market. Calculate the difference between the last price yesterday and the first price at the opening of the market to determine the size of the opening range. In this strategy, the most important aspect is the breakout; this is because it determines how far the price will move from the opening price.

Therefore, the opening range trade strategy uses the breakout range as the entry point and those who wish to enter trade should be keen enough to choose the correct point of entry.

During the early time of market opening, the breakout range is determined by the gap and the high or low breakthrough. When using this strategy, you need to direct your trade towards the breakout. However, as the day progresses, the breakouts should be seen as a caution. The stop-loss order is significant when using breakouts to trade in the morning, and when making estimates on how far you need to go, use the stop-loss order as the mid-point of the gap.

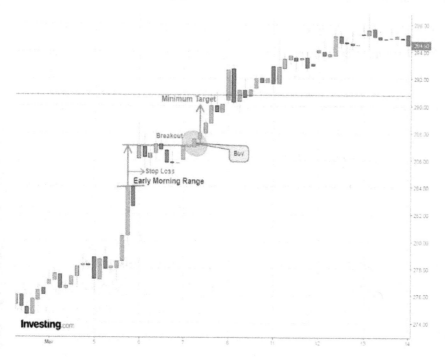

All the patterns discussed are useful in trading stock; it's important to understand them and know when to apply them to maximize profits. But if you find some of the work difficult to understand, it is good to master a few easier patterns and trade your way to greatness in the world of FOREX and stock trading.

Chapter 13: Day Trading Psychology

To be a successful day trader you need a certain mindset.

You must be positive. You need to start each day expecting to make good trades. There is no room for negativity in the trading room.

You must be intelligent. You should be able to analyze myriads of information and glean the important parts.

You must not be lazy. If you don't like recordkeeping, working a structured day, or following charts and trends, you won't like day trading. 80% of the workday is about routine, only 20% is thrills and excitement.

You must control your emotions. Trades must be based on logic, not intuition or hunches. Do not trade to reverse your losses. It won't work. You will lose more, possibly your entire trading account.

The market does not have a personal vendetta against you. This job is not personal. You must develop a thick skin because you'll have losses. They cannot affect your work ethic.

What is your plan for losses? You need a written plan for your behavior when you lose a trade. Practice your method of losing. Will you strike the wall and break your hand? Throw a pencil? Cry? Pound the desk? It would be much more effective if you just left the office for a break. Go to Starbucks and get a muffin and coffee.

Never take a bad mood home with you. Take a walk around the block, a workout at the gym, or go to a play, but do not let your workday affect your home life. Your family depends on you to be their physical and emotional support. If you're fixated on what happend at work, you aren't giving your family the 100% of your time they deserve.

Learn how to differentiate between your job performance and your personal identity. This is a crucial step for a day trader. If you don't, you'll go down in flames in the first year with emotional overload. Balance your life and your reactions to emotional events.

Some of the day-trading problems are not technique, but the emotional factor that makes a trade. The risk of losing trade can be debilitating with silence. Only one loss in the future will stop you from making other successful trades. Don't let this loop catch up with you. If you're making a losing trade, so what, you've reached your stop-loss (we 're going to talk about this later), and you're protected. You'll be making a lot of successful trades with our system, and you won't even notice the ones you miss because they'll be too low in comparison.

Poor risk management is probably one of the most important lessons that you, as a day trader, need to learn. Before you enter a trade, it is imperative that you know where you stand. There's no point in entering and hoping that the trade will suddenly take off and make you a millionaire throughout the night. That is not the way it happens. You have your finances to manage, how much can you lose? How much will you lose every week, until your finances are affected? Keep a record of any trade you do good or bad, sum it up at the end of every week. Once you put that into practice, day-to-day trade will be a lot easier.

We all want to get rich very fast, and yes it can be done, but only if you put your mind to it. Jumping into a trade & hoping it'll go up isn't the answer. Invest in a good course of trading & schedule every trade well in advance & know your exit strategy off by heart. Freezing while making a trade. Will I go in, or will I not go inside? That's a really hard emotion to deal with. You're waiting to see if the stock is rising & you 're too late to get in and before you know it's gained 5 percent. You're going to be patting yourself on the back & telling yourself you've been right about that stock & you're definitely going into it tomorrow. Of course, the next day, you do the same, always watching the stock rise but never committing to a deal.

While many men and women go into day-to-day trading to make a fast million, an amazing 2/3rds average of them will go away with some serious losses. Why do so many fail to gain with the enormous money-making potential associated with day-trading? Well, a quick look at the psychology of day trading gives some interesting answers to this question.

Psychology Affecting Traders' Habits

Psychological aspects affect habits in trading, the mistakes, and the winning strategies that a trader comes up with. Explained below are the negative habits that many traders make, with the influence of psychology on their habits.

Trading without a Strategy

With no trading strategy and plan, a trader will face challenges with no place to refer to for the anticipated result. A proper strategy should be drawn by a trader to be a referencing point when facing a problem in trading in the market. It should be a clearly constructed plan, detailing what to do in certain situations and which type of trading patterns to employ in different case scenarios. Trading without a strategy is akin to trading to lose your money.

Lack of Money Management Plans

Money management plans are one of the main aspects of trading, and without solid strategies in this, it's difficult to make progress in making gains in the trades opened. As a trader, you have to abide by certain principles that will guide you in how to spend your money in the account in opening up trades and ensuring that profits ensue from that.

Wanting to Always Be Right

Some traders always go against the market, placing their desire of what manner they would like the market to behave in. They don't follow the sign that the market points to, but rather they follow their own philosophy, not doing proper analysis and always wanting to be right.

Snapshot

No matter what the consequences, human nature is to defend itself. Effective day trading, however, allows traders to take significant daily risks. The consequence is bad choices that eventually cost a lot of money when basic human instinct tells you to go against the herd and quick trading rules that are necessary for successful deals.

Stay focused

Day trading psychology demystifies the erratic behavior of some traders by explaining how the stress and uncertainty our brains, bodies, and emotions deal with. When there are several emotions and perceptions are also swirling around in the investor's mind in the middle of volatile currency exchange or stock sale. In the face of such turmoil, people may tend to "cope" with the situation by losing focus and distracting themselves from the plan of logical and decisive action that your personal trading rules call for. This escape strategy costs a lot of money to many traders, as efficient stock purchases & sales or currency exchange demands fast and concentrated decisions in the heat of the moment.

Fear and Day Trading

Fear can work in both directions, as a limit to an overtrade, or also as a limit to making profits. A trader may close a trade to avert a loss, the action motivated by fear. A trader may also close a trade too early, even when on a winning streak in making gains, in fear that the market will reverse and that there will be losses. In both scenarios, fear is the motivator, working in avoiding failure a success at the same time.

The Fear to Fail

The fear to fail in trading may inhibit a trader from opening trades, and just watch as the market changes and goes in cycles when doing nothing. This fear is an inhibitor to success. It prevents a trader from executing what could have been a successful trade.

The Fear to Succeed

This type of fear in trading psychology will make a trader lose out his profits to the market when there was an opportunity to do otherwise. It works in a self-harming way in the market scenarios. Such traders in this category fear having too much profit and allow losses to run, all the while aware of their activities and the losses they are going to make.

The technical progress has made it possible for news to travel quick and reach far-flung places. This has created a unique situation for stock markets, where the positive news has a quick and positive reaction in the stock markets; but negative news causes sudden and a steep drop in stock prices as traders become gripped by fear and panic.

In situations leading to greed, traders still pause and think, if they are being greedy. But under the influence of fear, traders usually overreact and exit their position quickly. This has a chain-reaction effect on markets. Prices fall, traders sell in fear; prices fall further, traders sell more in fear. This creates bigger ripples in stock markets than greed does. Traders exit from their positions fearing that they will lose their profits or make losses. The fear of loss paralyzes novice traders when their positions turn into loss-making. They refuse to exit such positions, hoping for a bounce back in markets. What should have been a small loss, eventually turns into a big one for them, sometimes even wiping out their all trading capital. A rationally thinking person will quickly exit from such a position. But fear is such strong emotion in day trading, that it stops even rational people from taking correct decisions.

Technology can help traders make the right decision in such situations. Automated trading is one aspect of trading that eliminates emotional content from day trading. But automated trading software is expensive and not every trader can afford those. So, the next best thing is to take the help of stop and limit orders. Based on your trading plan, decide what will be your trade entry, exit, stop-loss and profit booking levels. To stop yourself from trading before the trade entry point has arrived, put a limit order for that level. It will free you from watching the price constantly. And, if you aren't watching markets constantly, the chance of wrong trading is also removed.

You cannot remove emotions from life. They will remain a part of your day trading business. But you can control it by self-discipline and proper trade management techniques. Patience is also one such technique, where you stay away from trading until the right trade entry level arrives.

Day-Trading Money Management and How it Affects Your Psychology

Control of capital is very critical at Day-Trading. The golden rule of Warren Buffet was to protect your resources, and this must be practiced in Day-Trading.

In Day-Trading, the use of a stop-loss is normally used to protect your trading capital or trading bank.

It's important that you also have a profit target. That means you have a predetermined maximum loss as well as a preset level of profit.

Dave, a Skilled E minis Day-Trader thinks it's compulsory to have a loss ratio of at least two to one income. That is, at least twice what your stop-loss is, is your profit goal.

This is crucial because if your profit goal and stop-loss are the same, it means at least 70 percent of the time, you need to get it right to make some money. Though, if you have a ratio of two to one, even if you only get it right 50 percent of the time, you still make a lot of money.

More importantly, it makes it very hard to lose money by having this two to one ratio. More than 70 percent of the time, you need to get it wrong to start losing money.

Another important part of money management is getting Day-Trading started with a small amount of money. You are likely to make mistakes when first learning, so it's better to make a mistake with a little bit of money rather than a lot. If you make a mistake with a small amount of money, you're likely to continue, but with a large amount of money, you will feel a lot of pain and thus stop trading, never learning from your mistake.

Starting with a big sum is risky and brings a lot of potential harm and this will greatly affect how you trade. In this case, the placing of trade causes great emotion. You may not even be able to place it as you are overwhelmed by your emotions.

You can also start worrying about the consequences of losing and focusing on the negative by using a large amount of money, which causes pressure on your emotions. In fact, this will create that reality to come about.

If you focus or worry about the consequences of losing, if you have a few losses, which is inevitable when trading, then you'll start to guess yourself and put your system in second place. This will then mean you 're going to make mistakes, not taking trades you're supposed to be taking or cutting short winning trades and fulfilling what you're focusing on.

The same can happen in the opposite direction. If you start using a large amount of money and you have some winning trades, you can get cocky and start trades in places that aren't really there, "close enough," and hence mess up your signals and trading system.

This allows you to start with a very small amount of money by Day-Trading using E mini Futures. At your account, you can start with as little as $2,000.

At this level, you start with just one contract in which you risk only $50 to make $100 for each trade. This is a level that most people can afford to start, and it can be handled by their psychology.

After that, you will build up your trading account slowly, and the sum you risk. So, $10,000 per month or more within a year is attainable.

Bias in Trading

There are several market biases that a trader may tend to make that may be as a result of emotions play, which traders are advised against. In the psychology of trading, these biases may influence a trader to make unwise and uncalculated trading decisions that may prove to be loss-making ones. Even when the trading biases are in focus, as a trader, you have to be aware of the emotions in you and come up with ways to keep them in check and maintain a cool head in your trading window.

Greed

It is common for traders to have their emotions and feelings jumbled up when day trading, from the highs and the lows they experience from the market. This is a far cry from the confident self that a trader usually poses before the markets open, bubbling up with excitement over the money and profits that they intend to make. Emotions in trading can mess up and impair your judgment, taking your ability to make wise decisions. Day trading is not to be carried out without emotions, but rather as a trader. You should know how to work your way around them, making them work for your good. A levelheaded and stable mind should always be maintained, whether your profits are on the rise, or whether you are on a losing streak. As a trader, you are not to disconnect from your emotions.

A trader may be fueled to earn more money by checking their balances in their accounts and seeing it be as of a low level. While this may be a motivator to work hard, some traders take it too far, wanting to earn a lot of money right there and then. They make mistakes while trading that has reverse effects than the intended ones ...

Taking Unnecessary Risks

Greed for more money will seek to convince the trader to take unworthy risks to achieve a certain financial threshold in the trading account. These will most likely end up in losses. The risky traders may take risks such as high leverage, and hope that will work in their favor, but at the same time may have them making huge losses.

Making an Overtrade

Due to the urge to make more and more money, a trader may extend over long periods of time trading. Commonly these efforts are to naught, for overtrading through the highs and the lows of the market put a trader in a position where their accounts can be wiped off as a result of greed. Not putting into account, the time of trading and plunging into opening trades without having done an analysis will most likely result in a loss.

Improper Profit and Loss Comprehension

Wanting to earn a lot of money within a short period of time will have a trader not closing a trade that is losing, maintaining the losses, and on the other hand, overriding on profit-making trade until a reverse in the market happens, canceling out all the gains made.

Conclusion

In the course of your trading experience, you must endeavor to learn from your adventures which is the most effective way to master a skill. Although a mentor or a teacher can help you, you will soon find out that the most influential opinion when trading is your own opinion so you must pay good attention to it and make it better. How can you make your opinion better? You can do this by possessing the right mentality when starting a trade. Whether the trade worked out or not, you must be ready to pick up yourself after losing a trade and focus again on the fact that you can make it again when trading next time. Having said that, you should also consider hiring a coach or get a mentor, someone who can always guide you in times when you experience difficulties in your trades. I hope you have been able to learn some simple yet effective strategies that will help you achieve success in your swing trading journey. Remember, always adhere to your strategy and be disciplined when trading.

I wish the best of luck in your trading.

SCAN ME

CPSIA information can be obtained
at www.ICGtesting.com
Printed in the USA
BVHW090008080621
608941BV00004B/1227